LIFE WITH CANCER

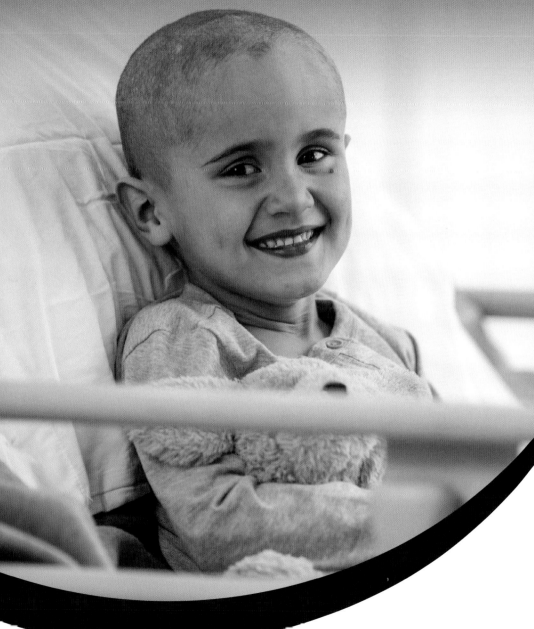

BY LINDSAY WYSKOWSKI

The Child's World®
childsworld.com

Published by The Child's World®
1980 Lookout Drive • Mankato, MN 56003-1705
800-599-READ • www.childsworld.com

Content Consultant: Julie Gralow, M.D., Jill Bennett Endowed Professor of Breast
Medical Oncology and Professor of Global Health, University of Washington School of
Medicine

Photographs ©: iStockphoto, cover, 1, 16; Shutterstock Images, 5, 6, 10; Monkey
Business Images/Shutterstock Images, 8; Fang Xia Nuo/iStockphoto, 12; Francis
Black/iStockphoto, 14; Buda Mendes/Getty Images Sports/Getty Images, 18; John
Kellerman/Shutterstock Images, 20

ISBN 9781503825079
LCCN 2017959681

Printed in the United States of America
PA02375

TABLE OF CONTENTS

FAST FACTS

- The human body is made up of cells. When cells are unhealthy and attack other parts of the body it is called **cancer**.

- Cancer is an illness that can affect anyone at any age. Children usually have different kinds of cancer than adults.

- Doctors don't know why people get cancer. They are trying to learn more about the body's cells and how to keep them healthy. Unlike a cold, you can't catch cancer from someone else.

- There are many kinds of cancer, so there are different ways to treat it. Drug therapy, **radiation**, and surgery are ways doctors try to stop cancer. Treatment can last for weeks or months. It is important that people build up their **immune system** before getting extreme treatment.

- In 2016, more than 15 million people living in the United States had been diagnosed with cancer.

CANCER TYPES

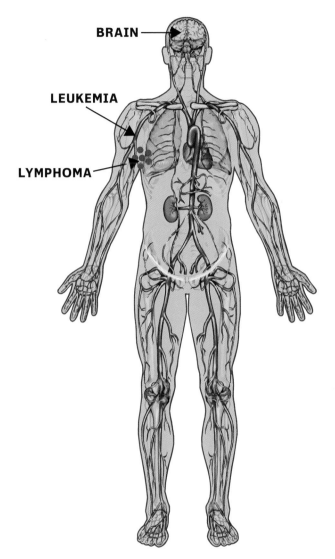

BRAIN

LEUKEMIA

LYMPHOMA

The most common types of cancer in children ages 0–14 are leukemia (cancer of the blood), cancer of the brain and other parts of the central nervous system, and lymphomas (cancer of the immune system). More than one-half of children diagnosed with cancer will be affected by one of these.

Chapter 1

THE DIAGNOSIS

Ted was the fastest runner in sixth grade. He won all the races against his classmates. Ted had yellow shoes with green laces, and he felt fast wearing those shoes.

One day, his body started feeling achy, and it hurt to run. Ted felt tired all the time. Even in his yellow shoes, he didn't want to run against his friends. Ted's teacher asked him how he felt. Ted told her his legs hurt so badly he couldn't think. He didn't feel like himself. The next day, Ted's dad took him to the doctor.

The doctor asked lots of questions and checked Ted's body. Ted had to have a blood test. This is used to test the blood for diseases that are not visible to the eye. The doctors used needles to access Ted's blood.

◄ **Even kids who are really active and healthy can get sick with cancer.**

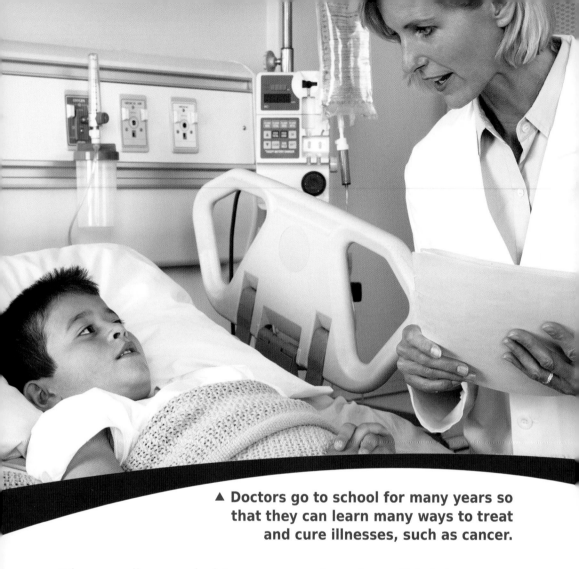

▲ Doctors go to school for many years so that they can learn many ways to treat and cure illnesses, such as cancer.

The needles made him nervous, but they didn't hurt too much.

The doctor asked Ted and his dad to step into his office. He was very serious. The doctor told Ted his blood tests were not normal. The tests showed Ted had leukemia, a cancer of the blood.

The next day, Ted and his parents met with the **oncologist**. She gave the family more information about what was happening to Ted's body. Ted needed to stay in the children's cancer wing at the hospital. He wanted to go home, but he had to have more tests to see how much of the cancer was in his body. Ted would start treatment immediately. He was scared, but he trusted that the doctors would make him feel better.

TYPES OF TREATMENT

Chemotherapy is one common treatment for cancer. It sometimes goes into a body through an IV or a port. Other times, it can be taken as a pill. Chemotherapy kills unhealthy cells throughout the whole body. Radiation is another way to stop unhealthy cells. Radiation uses a high-energy ray to stop the cancer in a specific area of the body. Doctors may also perform surgery to remove the cancer if the cancer cells are located in one contained spot in the body.

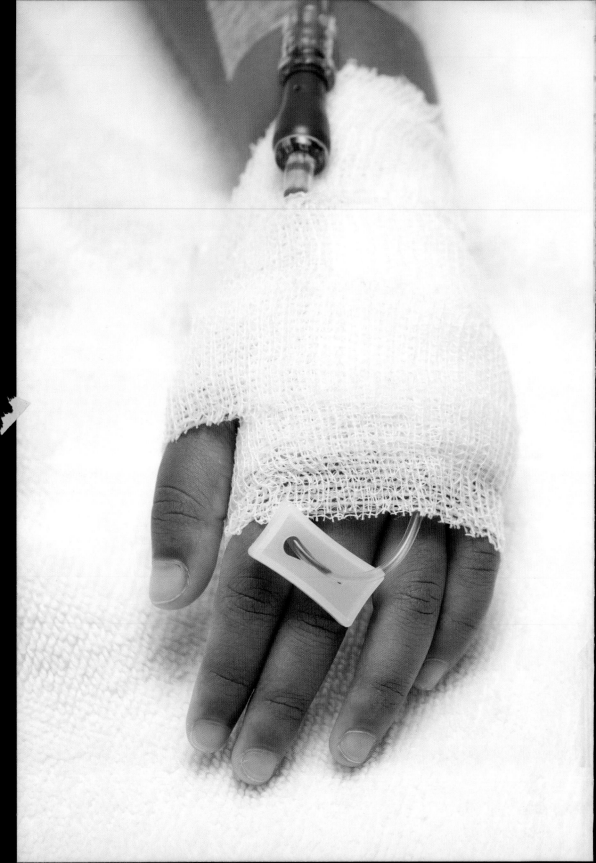

Chapter 2

A HOSPITAL VISIT

Seven-year-old Mary had been to the hospital many times for cancer treatments. Today, Mary's mom let her pick the music for the car ride to the hospital. Mary nodded her head to the music but didn't feel like singing.

Mary didn't always like going to the hospital. Sometimes it was scary and cold. Even though the nurses were kind and friendly, Mary wished she were back at home, where it was quiet and warm.

Mary wore brown boots and carried a brightly colored quilt from her grandma. The quilt helped her stay warm while she was at the hospital. Her blanket was cozy and reminded her of home.

◄ **Many treatments at the hospital include putting an intravenous needle into the arm. This needle enters the vein directly.**

When Mary arrived at the hospital, the doctors gave her medicine. Mary was undergoing a cancer-fighting treatment called chemotherapy. It was very strong and sometimes made Mary feel sick. Before the doctors gave her the chemotherapy, Mary took **anti-nausea medicine**.

The chemotherapy went into Mary's chest through a port. A port is a small metal disc that fits under the skin. A small tube goes from the port to a vein in the body. Then a needle goes through that tube into the bloodstream. Mary pretended she was a robot and the port was her charger.

At the hospital, Mary saw some therapy dogs. The dogs were trained to help support people who may have a sickness. Mary liked the dogs; they made her feel calm. The dogs gave Mary the extra strength she needed to fight against her cancer.

◄ **Sometimes kids have to stay in the hospital for a few days while they get treatment.**

Chapter 3

BACK TO SCHOOL

O llie was wearing his favorite blue shirt and had a big smile on his face. He was going back to school today. He hadn't been at school for a while because he had cancer. He spent a lot of time at the hospital getting treatments.

Ollie missed his friends and their class fish. He liked school. His favorite part was science. He wanted to be an astronaut when he grew up. But first, he had to work on building a strong immune system. With a strong immune system, Ollie could help fight off the cancer cells better.

When Ollie first got cancer, his mom came to school with him. She helped Ollie tell his fourth-grade class.

◀ **Doing homework at the hospital can be a good distraction for kids.**

▲ Kids can feel a little better during cancer treatment if they have a stuffed animal or toy that they love to keep them company.

They talked about cancer and how Ollie was going to miss school. He was still going to do his homework when he could.

Ollie tugged on his green hat. The hat was soft and kept his head warm. The hat also protected his head from the sun. Ollie had had shaggy blonde hair before, but now he was bald. His cancer treatment made his hair fall out. He knew one day it would grow back. Then maybe he could have a Mohawk.

Ollie's brother Tom gave him a lunchbox and they headed to school. Ollie felt the sun shining on his face and took a deep breath. He wasn't in **remission** yet, but he was glad to get back into a routine again.

HAIR LOSS AND CANCER

Sometimes people with cancer lose their hair because of their treatment. This happens because chemotherapy is so powerful. Sometimes it attacks good cells along with the bad ones, such as the cells that make hair. But not everyone loses their hair. When people do lose their hair, sometimes they wear wigs. Wigs can be made to match someone's natural hair color, or they can be made in fun, bright colors.

Chapter 4

WORLD CHAMPION ATHLETE

Hailey looked down at the medal around her neck. She had won a gold medal at the triathlon world championship and was about to hear the U.S. national anthem. She pumped her fist in the air, and the crowd cheered.

Hailey won her triathlon with a leg **prosthesis**. When Hailey was 12, she was diagnosed with bone cancer in her leg. To remove the cancer, Hailey had surgery. She also had chemotherapy. Once the cancer was gone, Hailey had another surgery to reconstruct her leg.

Even though the doctors tried to rebuild Hailey's leg, it didn't feel like it did before she had cancer.

◀ **Hailey Danisewicz has won many medals at the Paralympics, which is a sporting event for people with disabilities.**

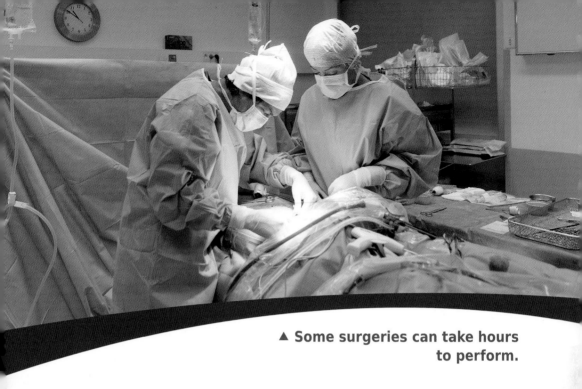

▲ **Some surgeries can take hours to perform.**

Sometimes Hailey felt pain in her leg. When she was 14, Hailey and her parents decided to have the doctors **amputate** her leg. This is usually an extreme solution. But Hailey and her family thought removing her leg was the best chance for her to be fully cured of the cancer.

Hailey had loved playing basketball and swimming. When she lost her leg, Hailey didn't know if she would play sports again.

When Hailey got older, one of her friends asked her to do a triathlon, a sport that combines swimming, biking, and running. Hailey realized she was really fast.

Hailey found a sport she loved, and soon she went to the world championships. Hailey now calls herself a cancer survivor and a world champion.

Hailey wants kids who have cancer to know they can still try new things. She visits children's hospitals to talk to the cancer patients. She hopes to give them a little hope during their stay.

THINK ABOUT IT

- How would you show support for a family member or friend who has cancer?
- What do you think would be the most difficult part of cancer treatments, and how would you keep a positive attitude?
- Imagine you are a cancer survivor. How would your outlook on life be different from someone who did not have to fight cancer?

GLOSSARY

amputate (AM-pyuh-tate): To amputate means to remove someone's arm or leg when it is unhealthy. Hailey's doctors needed to amputate the part of her leg that had been affected by cancer.

anti-nausea medicine (AN-ti-NAW-zhuh MED-uh-suhn): Anti-nausea medicine is medicine that helps stop the feeling of needing to throw up. Mary took anti-nausea medicine to help her feel less sick after chemotherapy.

cancer (KAN-sur): Cancer is a disease that spreads through unhealthy cells attacking healthy cells throughout the body. Ted was ill with cancer.

chemotherapy (kee-moh-THAYR-uh-pee): Chemotherapy is a medicine made up of strong chemicals that can kill cancerous cells. Mary had chemotherapy at the hospital.

immune system (i-MYOON SISS-tuhm): The immune system is a system of the body that keeps people healthy. When Ollie got sick, his immune system became weak and needed time to grow strong again.

oncologist (ong-KOL-uh-gyst): An oncologist is a doctor who specializes in cancer. Ted and his parents met with the oncologist after his diagnosis.

prosthesis (pross-THEE-sis): A prosthesis is an artificial limb, such as an arm or a leg. Hailey had a prosthesis for her leg.

radiation (ray-dee-AY-shuhn): Radiation is a high-energy ray, such as an x-ray. Ollie had radiation when he was sick.

remission (ri-MISH-uhn): Remission is what doctors call the period of time after the cancer is totally gone from the body. Ollie went into remission.

TO LEARN MORE

Books

Fcad, Beverlye Hyman. *Nana, What's Cancer?* Atlanta, GA: American Cancer Society, 2010.

Filigenzi, Courtney. *My Cancer Days.* Atlanta, GA: American Cancer Society, 2016.

Squire, Ann O. *Cancer.* New York, NY: Children's Press, 2016.

Web Sites

Visit our Web site for links about cancer.

childsworld.com/links

Note to Parents, Teachers, and Librarians: We routinely verify our Web links to make sure they are safe and active sites. So encourage your readers to check them out!

SELECTED BIBLIOGRAPHY

"Cancer in Children." *American Cancer Society.* American Cancer Society, Inc., 2017. Web. 4 Dec. 2017.

Keene, Nancy. *Childhood Cancer Survivors: A Practical Guide to Your Future.* Bellingham, WA: Childhood Cancer Guides, 2012. Print.

Woznick, Leigh A. *Living with Childhood Cancer: A Practical Guide to Help Families Cope.* Worcester, MA: American Psychological Association, 2002. Print.

INDEX

ABOUT THE AUTHOR

Lindsay Wyskowski is a writer and lifelong reader from Michigan. She has a master's degree in public relations and worked within the Olympic Movement for eight years. She loves to travel and experience new cultures.